Angus&Robertson
An imprint of HarperCollins*Publishers,* Australia

First published 1978 by William Collins Pty Ltd Sydney
First published in paperback 1982
Reprinted in 1984, 1985, 1987, 1990
This Bluegum paperback edition 1993
Reprinted 1996
by HarperCollins*Publishers* Pty Limited
ACN 009 913 517
A member of the HarperCollins*Publishers* (Australia) Pty Limited Group

Copyright © Percy Trezise and Dick Roughsey 1980

This book is copyright.
Apart from any fair dealing for the purposes of private study, research, criticism or review, as permitted under the Copyright Act, no part may be reproduced by any process without written permission.
Inquiries should be addressed to the publishers.

HarperCollins*Publishers*
25 Ryde Road, Pymble, Sydney, NSW 2073, Australia
31 View Road, Glenfield, Auckland 10, New Zealand
77-85 Fulham Palace Road, London W6 8JB, United Kingdom
Hazelton Lanes, 55 Avenue Road, Suite 2900, Toronto, Ontario M5R 3L2
and 1995 Markham Road, Scarborough, Ontario M1B 5M8, Canada
10 East 53rd Street, New York NY 10032, USA

National Library of Australia Cataloguing-in-Publication data:

Trezise, Percy.
Banana bird and the snake men.
ISBN 0 207 18148 9
[1.] Aborigines, Australian–Legends–Juvenile literature.
I. Roughsey, Dick. II. Title.
398.210994

Typeset by Savage & Co., Brisbane
Printed in Hong Kong

6 5 4 3 2   96 97 98 99

Banana Bird and the Snake Men

written and illustrated by

PERCY TREZISE & DICK ROUGHSEY

Angus&Robertson
An imprint of HarperCollins*Publishers*

In Dreamtime, in the very beginning, people who were to become birds, animals, plants and reptiles, were still in human form.

The Snake men of the Cape York wilderness were cannibals. They would kill people, hang them in trees, and collect them later when they were hungry.

The Snake men were able to change themselves into kangaroos, so they could travel faster and further.

When they did this their eyes turned red. This meant that they were very bad men.

One hot, dry day, when the Snake men had changed into red kangaroos, they went down to a lily lagoon to drink.

A party of Bird men were out hunting. They saw the kangaroos and decided to spear them. They did not know they were the bad Snake men.

Banana Bird man speared the largest kangaroo, who was really the Taipan Snake man.

Taipan Snake man pulled the spear from his flank, then smelt it to discover who had speared him. He began sniffing all around.

All the Snake men now began knocking the trees down, jumping this way and that. But Banana Bird man kept moving from tree to tree, always just in front of them.

Finally Banana Bird man climbed into a lady-apple tree which was very strong. By now the Snake men were so tired they couldn't knock down another tree.

When the Snake men found they could not knock down the lady-apple tree, they changed themselves into snakes and hid in the long grass.

Banana Bird man stayed in the lady-apple tree all night, he was very frightened of the Snake men. He ate lots of ripe red and white apples.

Next morning Banana Bird man broke off some branches and threw them into the grass around the tree. He wanted to make sure that the Snake men had all left.

When he thought it was safe he climbed down slowly. He put one foot on the ground, looking carefully around. Still no sign of the Snake men. He put his other foot on the ground and straight away Taipan Snake man bit him.

Then all the Snake men came out of hiding and attacked Banana Bird man.
They tore him to pieces and then ate him.

After their big feed the Snake men lay down on the grass and went to sleep.

Coucal Bird man was the brother of Banana Bird man, and he came looking for him. He saw all the trees knocked over and looked about for tracks.

He found the remains of Banana Bird man under the lady-apple tree. Then he saw all the Snake men sleeping there.

Coucal Bird man ran back to his camp and told all the Bird men what had happened to his brother.

The women began to cut themselves with stones and wailed for Banana Bird man. The Bird men took up their firesticks and went off to kill the Snake men.

When the Bird men came to the sleeping Snake men they took their firesticks and lit the grass in a big circle around them.

The Snake men did not know that the fire was coming because it was magic fire which burned without making any smoke or noise.

The Snake men did not wake up until the fire was all around them. Five of them went underground.

But the others could find no way to escape. They threshed about and died.

All the Snake men were now dead, or travelling away underground.

The Bird men came back and sang up a storm to put the fire out.

The rain ran through the holes left by the five escaping Snake men.
They became the five rivers which flow from the low plateau now called
The Desert.

Grass will not grow there since that magic fire. And when the Bird people changed into all kinds of birds, they agreed to always warn each other when snakes are about.